The Sit Down Come Heel Stay and Stand Book

CLAIRE ARROWSMITH

tfh

CREDITS

T.F.H. Publications, Inc.
One TFH Plaza
Third and Union Avenues
Neptune City, NJ 07753

Printed and bound in China
08 09 10 11 12 1 3 5 7 9 8 6 4 2

Library of Congress Cataloging-in-Publication Data
    Arrowsmith, Claire.
    The sit down come heel stay and stand book / Claire Arrowsmith.
        p. cm.
    Includes index.
    ISBN 978-0-7938-0660-7 (alk. paper)
    1. Dogs--Training. I. Title.
    SF431.A77 2008
    636.7'0887--dc22
                2008001905

tfh

The Leader in Responsible Animal Care for Over 50 Years!™
www.tfh.com

CENTRAL *Garden & Pet*

CLAIRE ARROWSMITH

Claire Arrowsmith is a full member of the Association of Pet Behavior Counsellors (APBC) and holds an Honors degree in Zoology and a Masters degree in Applied Animal Behavior and Animal Welfare. She worked with rescue animals and was the behaviorist at Hearing Dogs for Deaf People before beginning her own behavior practice. She now focuses on behavior problems in pet dogs and cats and also offers training advice. Claire is a qualified Puppy School tutor and runs popular dog training classes and is the specialist behaviorist for Houndstar Films DVDs on dog breed information.

She features in her own '*Puppy Training*', '*Trick Training*' and '*Banishing Bad Behaviour*' DVDs. Claire features on the expert panel of *Your Dog* magazine providing answers to readers' questions and presents regular advisory talks about problem dogs. Claire has shared her home with a multitude of pets including hamsters, rats, cats and dogs and was brought up in the Highlands of Scotland surrounded by a range of farm animals, working dogs and wildlife which fuelled her love of, and interest in, all animal behavior. She currently lives with her husband and rescue Rhodesian Ridgeback mix dog, Sarnie.

CONTENTS

THE SIX ESSENTIAL TRAINING DISCIPLINES

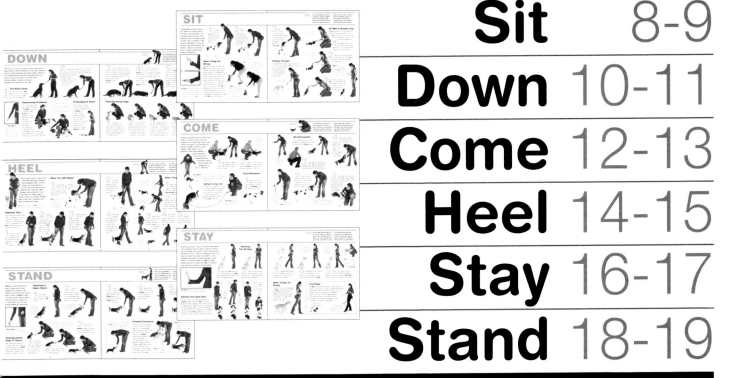

8 PAGE FOLD-OUT TRAINING ACHIEVEMENT RECORD

INTRODUCTION

Training your dog can seem quite daunting at first, so this book has been produced to show you how easy it can be to achieve success with the six staple commands: **Sit, Down, Come, Heel, Stay** and **Stand**. You'll learn the basic steps for each command in a simple and structured way which will make it easier for you and your dog to achieve success. Each exercise is accompanied by step-by-step photographs that show you clearly what should be happening at every stage of the process.

The training methods are described as 'positive' training because they use luring and non-forceful ways to get your dog to follow the command and focus upon rewards and verbal praise when your dog succeeds. This is a very enjoyable and fulfilling way to train – both for you and also for your dog. (See pages 24-27 for training tips.)

Left Playing games can be a great way to build a bond, reward successful training and to keep your dog eager and motivated.

THE LESSON PLAN

Each obedience command is presented on its own double-page spread for you to follow. It is advisable to begin with the '**Sit**' as your first command and then work your way through each one at your own pace. You will see the breakdown of each command in detail and will be given tips to help you overcome potential

CHARTING YOUR PROGRESS

FOLD-OUT SIDE ONE

To help you keep track of your progress and to give you goals to aim for while training, you will find a pull-out **Training Chart** at the back of the book. You should work through each step at your own pace and make sure that your dog can easily and consistently perform the task before you move on to the next stage. Don't expect to move through

GETTING THE BEST FROM YOUR TRAINING

FOLD-OUT SIDE TWO

How long it will take to train your dog to learn each command depends upon your experience, your dog's age, its breed and character, and the amount of time you dedicate to training. Try to stick consistently to your training rules and practice several times a day during normal daily interactions with your dog, such as petting, feeding or walking times. Results will be slower if you only train a few times a week and allow your dog to do as he pleases for the remaining time.

problems as you train. The methods are suitable for all ages and breeds of dogs. Some dogs have health problems that may cause them pain or discomfort (such as when the dog performs particular movements or eats certain foods), so in those cases it is best to seek advice from your vet before training, even though all the methods described in the book are co-operative and avoid the use of force.

The training plans take you through all the necessary steps and suggest tips to help you achieve success with each command.

each command at the same speed. Each individual command should be practiced and perfected in its own time. Different dogs will have different strengths and weaknesses and yours may be better at doing some things than others. This is perfectly normal and just means that you need to focus more time on those tasks that are not so simple to conquer.

The training plan is split into three Achievement Stages. When you and your dog progress through each of these stages, you can mark your success in each of the six commands by sticking on the stars and ribbons that can be found opposite page 28.

If your dog has a behavioral problem, such as a fearful or aggressive disposition, which makes it hard to groom or handle him, then seek advice to deal with this before trying to embark on a training plan. Take your time and always reward your dog for his calm, friendly behavior. The training itself should help to build a good relationship between you and help you to resolve any confusion.

Training your dog should be fun and enjoyable for you both. If done correctly, it should strengthen your bond while teaching your dog to become well-behaved and reliable.

PUPPY TRAINING

If you have a very young puppy you can still follow the training plan since it uses kind and simple techniques. Puppies learn very quickly so it's best to get them into good habits as early as possible. Since very young dogs can find it hard to concentrate for long, it's important to try to train for just a few minutes per session. Then allow your puppy to relax, perhaps by resting, having a break outside or playing with toys. As he grows up, his ability to concentrate will gradually improve.

SIT

A reliable **Sit** command should be a priority for all dog owners. This basic command allows you to promote *good manners, calm behavior* and is the starting point for many other commands. A **Sit** is easily achievable but ensuring that your dog will respond in *any* situation, without you having to shout or repeat yourself, takes patience and practice.

1 Encourage your dog to approach you. Let him sniff at a treat held in your hand but don't let him eat it.

2 Slowly move your hand up so your dog's head tips up as he follows the treat. His bottom will naturally move downwards.

*Sit Signal This gesture comes from the upward movement made while luring your dog into position. He will associate the movement, even with an empty hand, with the **Sit**.*

When Things Go Wrong

Although a simple command, the **Sit** sometimes goes wrong. Luckily problems are easily solved. Always train in a quiet, comfortable area where your dog can focus. If you find that your dog jumps up, then you need to check the position of the treat. Make sure your lure is close to his nose and not too high as a raised treat might encourage him to jump. If your dog knows the **Sit** but breaks from the position too soon, then practice keeping his focus on you while delaying the arrival of the reward slightly. He'll learn that staying in the **Sit** brings more rewards.

Left It's easy to accidentally teach a dog to jump rather than sit by holding the treat just above his head but still within his reach.

Right By raising the signal a little higher this dog stops jumping and sits correctly. Wait for the right position before rewarding.

This can be taught very quickly provided you practice regularly. Begin to ask your dog to **Sit** before you put his bowl down or put on the collar and leash. If he gets up, put him back in position before continuing. Outside, you can introduce the **Sit** before crossing streets, but be patient if he is worried by passing traffic.

3 The moment your dog's bottom touches the floor release the treat and praise. If rewarded, your dog will quickly learn a reliable **Sit**.

Staying Focused

Everyone finds that their dog is distracted from time to time during training. If your dog ignores your lure, then he might have had too many treats already or you may need more enticing treats.

Vary your treats and keep training sessions short.

Try not to lean over your dog as you train.

Training at his level helps to build a young dog's confidence.

Sit With A Smaller Dog

Training a puppy or a small adult dog uses the same principles as with larger dogs. Be very aware of your own movements so that you don't inadvertently alarm him.

1 If possible, kneel down with your dog or at least arrange it so you can reach him without towering over him.

2 Slowly lure his head up and back using very careful hand movements. Small dogs require more precision.

*Right Practice until your dog quickly responds to the **Sit** hand signal or verbal command when you're in a standing position.*

3 As your dog sits, say '**Sit**' so he makes the right association. Always wait until he's correctly in position before rewarding.

DOWN

Teaching your dog to lie down is easy and does *not* require force. These methods use your dog's ability to read *your* body language and hand signals. Most of us naturally gesture towards the ground when we want our dogs to lie down so it seems like common sense to teach your dog to recognize that signal from the start.

1 The Basic Down

Start with your dog in a **Sit** position in front of you. Hold a treat to your dog's nose and allow him to sniff it without releasing it.

2

Keeping the treat close to the nose, very slowly move it straight down between his front paws so his nose follows it downwards. Be patient and use steady movements and you'll find that he bends over in attempt to get the food.

Down Signal

Your hand signal will develop from the basic lure movement towards the ground into a simple downwards gesture.

Overcoming Problems

Some dogs take longer than others to master the **Down**. If your dog is having trouble, **don't** resort to pushing or pulling him into position. This may detract from his enjoyment of the training. Be patient and make sure you're practicing in a place where your dog is relaxed, on a soft surface, and that you reward every success.

If your dog's bottom rises up, sit on the floor and lure him under your outstretched leg. He'll lie down to follow the food, which gives you the chance to reward and reinforce the position.

Prolonging A Down

Some dogs get up as soon as they've been rewarded. Initially, prolong the **Down** by swiftly offering another reward before he moves. Hiding a treat under your foot can be a good way to quickly reveal a reward for staying **Down** obediently.

If your young dog is very energetic or you are training around distractions, start by using his leash to provide control. Step on the leash, ensuring it allows him some movement, and then lure him down.

3 Your dog will find himself hunched over and will move his feet to rebalance. Keep your hand in position and avoid the temptation to move it. Since this position is not easy for your dog to hold, a **Down** comes naturally.

4 As soon as you see your dog is flat on the floor, say '**Down**' and offer the treat immediately. By introducing your verbal command just as he gets the position right, your dog will find it easier to link the word with the **Down** position.

5 As you practice the **Down** command, your dog will start to recognize the hand movement and move into position faster. You'll gradually be able to stand straighter to give your command.

Teaching Small Dogs

Take it slowly and steadily as you lure the dog down.

Give the reward when he's in the right position.

1 You will need to crouch down or, if this is hard to manage, start with your dog on the same level as you. Show your dog the treat (as described in the Basic Down).

2 Even small hand gestures can encourage huge movements in tiny dogs so hold your hand steady as you move it downwards. Remember to go slowly so he can follow.

3 Small dogs often lift their bottoms or manage to crouch instead of lying down. It's usually just a case of needing more practice and precision, but remember our problem tips.

4 Be patient, keep your hand steady and ignore the temptation to move it around. With well-timed praise and consistency, even the tiniest of dogs will learn the **Down** in no time.

COME

Owning a dog that does not reliably return while on a walk is a major cause for concern. It is vital that your dog is under control at all times so that he does not become a public nuisance, frighten people or their dogs or other pets. Coming back reliably is highly dependent upon dog-owner relationships and the breed instincts. Some breeds were designed to run and run, after all.

Your friend must avoid restraining the dog when he starts to run to you.

1 Start in a n enclosed area. Ask a friend to help by gently holding your dog by his collar while you tease him with a treat.

2 Then move away a short distance. Open your arms and call '**Come**', at which point he should be allowed to run to you.

Come Signal *This is particular to each owner and dog, though most dogs respond well to open arms and a happy face. This can be less exaggerated once your dog has learned to come back reliably.*

Using A Long Line

If you need extra confidence, you can use a long, trailing line that gives your dog freedom, but restricts how far he can move away from you until you are sure he responds consistently and well to your '**Come**' command.

Encourage your dog to return to you, rather than using the line to pull him back.

Extra Motivation

1 Some dogs much prefer a good game with a favorite toy than a tidbit. Use **whatever** gets him running to you fastest.

You should never punish your dog for being slow to return. If you do, he'll be even less inclined to return to you the next time you call 'Come.' If he's slow, then use a line and practice in quieter areas until he understands. Think hard about what really motivates your dog and make sure you're using the correct rewards.

Be Enthusiastic!

If you are serious, silent or look unfriendly, it is unlikely that you will succeed with the **Come** training.

Avoid calling your dog's name over and over.

3 He should start towards you. Keep calling him and respond enthusiastically to prevent him then becoming distracted and veering away.

4 Reward immediately and praise him when he arrives. As you offer the treat, gently take hold of his collar. This allows you to control whether he can rush away again.

2 When your dog arrives, you can play a game. It's a good idea to bring two toys, so you always have another to get his attention.

*You might want to save the toy just for taking on walks, so your dog is delighted to see it and **really** wants to play.*

Toy ropes or ones with squeakers can be very exciting. End the game before your dog is ready to keep him interested.

3 Even when you're playing, remember to keep praising your dog for coming back. Once he's got the idea, start to practice when he's playing with dogs or meeting other people.

HEEL

Most owners want to enjoy their walks with their dog. However, being dragged along, as and where your dog pleases, is not fun. Dogs that pull end up getting fewer walks and often develop other problems. Even small dogs can make walks a misery. Dogs can actually damage their throat, neck, shoulders and back by persistent pulling.

*Left Take time to teach the **Heel** command and you can both enjoy walks together.*

What You Will Need

1 A well-fitting comfortable collar. It should be loose enough so that you can still fit two fingers between the dog's neck and the collar itself.

***Right** Avoid collars that tighten up or pinch your dog. They aren't necessary for good behavior.*

Heelwork Plan

Dogs don't know that they are meant to walk next to you so you'll need to spend time teaching your dog that doing so is *really* rewarding. The **Heel** requires practice and consistency from you.

1 Get your dog's attention. Lure him into place beside you; either side is fine depending on what feels most comfortable.

2 While he is focused on you, move forwards one step. If he walks with you, say '**Heel**' and reward him before moving on a few more steps.

3 Keep praising your dog while the leash remains relaxed. Keep the treat ready to offer but be careful not to encourage jumping.

You must motivate your dog to **want** to walk with you. The world is very exciting and if you ignore him he will become distracted. It can sometimes feel a little awkward to interact with your dog in public (praising and offering treats), but being dragged along, having no control, is arguably more embarrassing.

When Things Go Wrong

2 A strong, leash, long enough to hold comfortably while allowing for some movement by the dog.

Pulling is most likely when the dog is starting his walk.

Lure rather than jerking the leash.

1 Almost all dogs will pull on the leash at some point during training. It's really important that he learns that pulling actually makes you **stop moving**. He'll then try hard to keep the leash loose.

2 Try not to pull your dog back towards you. Instead, encourage your dog back to you and lure him into place again. This means he does the work rather than you pulling him back or rushing to catch up.

4 Gradually build up the distance your dog walks before you offer the rewards. Start to practice around distractions, such as people or traffic.

3 When your dog is back beside you and focusing well, then continue walking and rewarding again.

4 Alternatively, you can try turning quickly and walking the opposite way when your dog pulls.

5 Your dog will have to catch up with you and in the process he forgets about pulling.

Walking next to you brings wonderful rewards for your dog.

Your dog must turn to follow.

STAY

Teaching your dog to stay in one place until released is an important task as it helps to keep him safe as well as instilling extra control. Owners often forget to practice this but it is vital for emergencies when your dog's movement may lead to accidents or injury (perhaps near roads), or frighten members of the public. It is helpful to think of a **Stay** as simply another training command that helps to stimulate your dog while you learn to work together.

Stay Signal *The natural gesture to signal 'Don't move' is usually a flat hand or a pointed index finger.*

Starting The Down Stay

1 Get your dog's focus and then place him in a **Down** position. Give your '**Stay**' command.
2 Turn and begin stepping away. Ensure success by building up the distance you move and the time he stays gradually. **3** Turn around and walk back to your dog. **4** Once you've returned, you can release your dog from the **Stay** by telling him "Release". Praise him well for mastering this important lesson.

Teaching The Sit Stay

1 Begin in the **Sit**. Give your hand signal and say '**Stay**' before pausing and rewarding your dog for remaining in place.

2 Give the command and slowly step away. Move only one step to begin with before returning and rewarding him.

An empty flat hand is a natural **Stay** *gesture.*

Move only one step to begin with.

Release your dog from his **Stay** *and then reward with his favorite petting or game.*

When your dog's **Stand** is over, you should release the food immediately. If you are slow or move the treats too far away from his nose before letting him eat them, he's likely to take several steps forward. If you reward late, you'll encourage him to move or walk forwards.

3 As he follows the food, your dog will be lured into the **Stand** position. As he gets up, command '**Stand**' and then reward him.

4 Build up the time your dog will **Stand** for you. Offer treats to keep him focused and happy about the task.

5 Practice regularly until your dog can **Stand** still while allowing you to examine him all over without moving.

Once your dog is confident with the **Stand**, *try practicing while you stand up and also in different places.*

A Useful Command

It's easy to become frustrated when your dog moves around while you try to handle him. The more irritated you are, the less calm your dog will be. Dogs that can **Stand** nicely and enjoy being touched will benefit from their owner noticing injuries or changes in body condition earlier. These dogs are often groomed more thoroughly too. Slowly build up the handling so your dog always feels comfortable.

Above *With practice, your dog should love being toweled off.*

Below *Keep your dog focused on the food in one hand while you begin grooming using a soft brush with the other.*

Step-by-Step Achievement Program

Carefully teach your dog the six lessons presented earlier in this book. Your dog's age, breed and character will influence how quickly he learns. You should expect him to find some tasks harder than others. Puppies normally learn very quickly and can master the basic commands within a few lessons. However, **don't try to rush** through the various levels too quickly as it might overwhelm or cause confusion. Older untrained dogs may take time to get used to using their brains but, by making it rewarding, every dog can make progress. Extra patience and consistency may be needed with new or rescued dogs.

For swift and reliable success **keep training sessions short** and try to fit in several sessions each day. Young pups respond well to regular training sessions lasting just a few minutes. Older dogs can learn a surprising amount in a couple of 20-minute sessions each day if they enjoy the lesson. The more training you fit into the day in a natural way, such as when offering the food bowl or putting on the leash, the faster your progress will be.

Three Stages To Success

The achievement program is divided into **three stages** giving you goals to aim for. Work through the plan in sequence (Stage One through to Stage Three) so that your dog has a clear understanding of the command. You can work on the six commands simultaneously. Keep practicing and you will earn the six ribbons and be the owner of **a well-trained dog**.

3 Moving on from Food Rewards

Don't worry that you'll have to walk around with pockets stuffed full of treats forever. Initially you should reward your dog every time he gets a new action right. This will encourage him to do the right thing again next time. However, when your dog has perfected the routine, you should begin to offer food on a more random basis, perhaps after every second or third correct response. You can still praise him each time. Your dog will keep trying to earn his treat so keep him guessing as to when the treat might arrive. Over time you should slowly reduce the amount of food rewards until you only use them now and again as a surprise.

4 Using Toys

Toys can also keep your dog interested and rewarded for training. They are harder to use for basic training since once your dog has the toy in his possession, you have to allow him time to play with it before getting it back. This can make training rather time-consuming. Toys are great for dogs that are not interested in food or for dogs that will do **anything** to get their ball! Picking a toy to suit your dog can be hard; think about texture, size, noise and movement, which are all characteristics that may or may not excite your dog. Test your dog with a range of suitable and safe items. He may prefer squeaky toys, soft toys, tuggy toys, bouncing ones – have fun finding out! Keep some toys special by putting them away in-between training sessions.

5 Good Timing

To get the most benefit from your reward, it needs to get to your dog within three seconds of the action you are encouraging. If you delay any longer than that, your dog will be confused about what you are training and might learn an undesirable action instead. Good timing is a skill that you will be practicing as you train your dog. Be clear in your mind what you are looking for and respond as soon as you see the desired action being performed.

	1	2	3	
Sit SEE LESSON ON PAGES 8-9	Your dog will '**Sit**' when you lure him into position with a treat. He can do this without jumping up at you.	You can stand up straight and give your **Sit** hand signal and your dog will respond reliably. You are still rewarding each time.	Your dog can sit consistently for the count of 10 before you reward him with a treat.	★
Down SEE LESSON ON PAGES 10-11	You can guide your dog into a **Down** position using a food lure.	You are standing straighter and your lure gesture does not go all the way to the floor before your dog responds.	Your dog can remain in the **Down** position for the count of 20.	☆
Come SEE LESSON ON PAGES 12-13		Your dog can run across a room when you call.	Your command '**Come**' gets a response from around the house and when in the yard.	☆
Heel SEE LESSON ON PAGES 14-15		Your dog can be lured next to you and will remain beside you while you take a few steps.	Your dog regularly looks up at you while walking and returns to your side if the leash goes tight.	☆
Stay SEE LESSON ON PAGES 16-17	Your dog has achieved level 3 in the **Sit** and **Down** lessons.		Your dog can remain in position while you take one step away from him and return.	☆
Stand SEE LESSON ON PAGES 18-19	You can lure your dog into a **Stand** position from a sit.	Your dog quickly stands when you give the hand signal.		☆